THOUGHTFULNESS THINKING

Growth Mindset

VICKY BUREAU
M.S., SCHOOL COUNSELING

A Starfish Book

SEAHORSE
PUBLISHING

Teaching Tips for Caregivers:

As a caregiver, you can help your child succeed in school by giving them a strong foundation in language and literacy skills and a desire to learn to read.

This book helps children grow by letting them practice reading skills.

Reading for pleasure and interest will help your child to develop reading skills and will give your child the opportunity to practice these skills in meaningful ways.

- Encourage your child to read on her own at home
- Encourage your child to practice reading aloud
- Encourage activities that require reading
- Establish a reading time
- Talk with your child
- Give your child writing materials

Teaching Tips for Teachers:

Research shows that one of the best ways for students to learn a new topic is to read about it.

Before Reading

- Read the "Words to Know" and discuss the meaning of each word.
- Read the back cover to see what the book is about.

During Reading

- When a student gets to a word that is unknown, ask them to look at the rest of the sentence to find clues to help with the meaning of the unknown word.
- Ask the student to write down any pages of the book that was confusing to them.

After Reading

- Discuss the main idea of the book.
- Ask students to give one detail that they learned in the book by showing a text dependent answer from the book.

TABLE OF CONTENTS

Growth Mindset: Do You Have It?

Do you know how to ice-skate?

Or catch a big fish?

Are you willing to learn a new skill?

Or does the worry of **failure** keep you from trying new things?

Sometimes, it's scary to try new things.

Sometimes, we don't even want to start.

But trying new things with a **growth mindset** helps us grow, learn, and build **confidence**!

Did you know that failure is the surest way to **success**?

After all, you weren't born knowing how to run!

In other words, it's okay to fall down as long as you get back up!

It’s okay to make mistakes.

That’s why pencils have erasers!

It’s okay to not know something.

As long as you are ready to learn!

7 + 3 = 10
9 + 3 = 12

Growth Mindset: What Does It Mean?

Will you try a new way to solve that difficult math problem?

10+22= 54+23=

24-14=

Having a growth mindset means that you are willing to fail, but hopeful about success.

Failure doesn't happen because you can't do it.

Failure happens when you stop trying.

It all depends on your **attitude**.

It might take a few tries.

You may fall a few times.

You may even want to give up.

But keeping a growth mindset is the only way to succeed.

It may not always be easy, but it's always worth it.

Because YOU are worth it!

Try some of this, or explore some of that.

Say more of this, or do less of that.

Look within YOU!

Growth Mindset: How Can You Build Yours?

How can you develop a growth mindset?

You can learn more about yourself! Want to know how?

Instead of thinking, “I can’t,” try thinking, “I can’t yet!”

Think less, “I won’t,” and more, “I will!”

So what if you didn’t get it right the first time? Or the second? Or the third?

Success takes time. And what’s the rush?

What Would You Do?

You still can't ice-skate. Do you practice at home, or return your skates?

Your schoolwork seems too hard. Do you ask for help, or give up?

Let's review your answers!

Learning a new skill can seem scary, but trying something unfamiliar can help to build confidence!

Learning new things can be frustrating, but all things are difficult before they become easy!

Words to Know

attitude (AT-i-tood): a person's way of thinking or feeling

confidence (KAHN-fuh-dens): a belief that you can succeed

failure (FAYL-yer): lack of success; falling short of expectations

growth mindset (grohth MIGHND-set): belief that success comes from effort; thinking in a hopeful, happy way

success (suhk-CESS): the accomplishment of a goal

Index

Comprehension Questions

1. How can you show a growth mindset even when things seem hard or difficult?

2. What are some things you can do to help you build a growth mindset?

3. How does a person's attitude affect their growth mindset?

4. What is the difference between failure and success?

About the Author

Vicky Bureau was born in Longueuil, Quebec, and was raised in South Florida. As a teacher, she developed a passion for the social and emotional growth of her students and later transitioned into the area of child and adolescent psychology after earning her master's degree in school counseling.
In addition to working with children, Vicky loves to be surrounded by animals and nature. She lives in Fort Lauderdale with her family: Billy, Khloe, M.J., and Max; her three cats, Alley, Baguette, and Salem; and her dog, Boomer.

Written by: Vicky Bureau
Design by: Under the Oaks Media
Editor: Kim Thompson

Photographs/Shutterstock: Benjavisa Ruangvaree: cover, p. 1; hedgehog94: p. 5; goodluz: p. 6-7; TinnaPong: p. 8; SviatlanaLaza: p. 9; Cheryl Casey: p. 11; Flamingo Images: p. 13; The Faces: p. 14; Rawpixel.com: p. 15; insta-photos: p. 16a; Jacob Lund: p. 16b; Arsenaii Palivoda: p. 17a; PXMedoa: p. 17b; KKTan: p. 19

Library of Congress PCN Data
Growth Mindset / Vicky Bureau
Thoughtfulness Thinking
ISBN 978-1-63897-096-5 (hard cover)
ISBN 978-1-63897-182-5 (paperback)
ISBN 978-1-63897-268-6 (EPUB)
ISBN 978-1-63897-354-6 (eBook)
Library of Congress Control Number: 2021945220

Printed in the United States of America.

Seahorse Publishing Company
www.seahorsepub.com

Published in the United States
Seahorse Publishing
PO Box 771325
Coral Springs, FL 33077